# SECRETARIAT: A 1970s SUPERSTAR

Written by A.J. Chilson

Illustrated by Earl Haughton

## DISCLAIMER

This book is not to be reprinted, reproduced or remanufactured, without the expressed consent of the author, who is also the publisher, of this book. "THOROUGHBRED PICAYUNE" is a fictitious newspaper created by the author.

## DEDICATION

To my late aunt Francis Hamacher (1945-2022), who had a love for horses. Her daughter (and my favorite cousin) Karen Deyke and I intend to honor Francis' memory by going to the Kentucky Derby.

There once was a racehorse who was not only big, but could run very fast. His name was Secretariat (pronounced Seh-Krah-Tear-E-It), and the fans loved him.[1]

---

[1] Secretariat was a big horse, bigger than most racehorses. His record-setting race times were said to be from him having a larger heart than most of his peers. When Secretariat died, a veterinarian (or animal doctor) performed a necropsy (or autopsy) on the horse. It was determined his heart was between 21 and 22 pounds. That's almost twice the size of a normal horse. Fans were amazed when they saw Secretariat run, either in-person or on television. They came to admire the horse, who would be visited by many after his career was over.

In this illustration, the man depicted guiding Secretariat was his horse groom, Eddie Sweat (1939-1998). Eddie understood Secretariat more than anyone else, and the horse trusted him. Eddie was one of the best grooms in horse racing for four decades.

To be a great racehorse, it helps that they have an owner who believes in them. Secretariat's owner was an elegant and graceful woman named Penny Chenery.[2]

---

[2]     Helen "Penny" Chenery (known during Secretariat's career by her married name at the time, Penny Tweedy; 1922-2017) inherited from her father Christopher Chenery a love for horses. Her goal in life was to own a successful racehorse. After working as a military designer and nurse during World War II, Penny took over Meadow Stable, a horse farm located near Ashland, Virginia. Under her leadership, Meadow Stable transformed from a failing business to a very successful one. Penny's dreams came true in 1972 when one of her horses, Riva Ridge, won two of the three "Triple Crown" events. But with Secretariat, Penny would become even more famous. She would be one of the most respected people in horse racing.

In 2010, Penny was portrayed by actress Diane Lane in the movie *Secretariat*.

A horse also needs to have a skilled trainer who loves horses to prepare them for a race. Secretariat had that in a Canadian named Lucien Laurin.[3]

---

[3] Born in the Canadian province of Quebec, Lucien Laurin (seen near the center of this illustration; 1912-2000) had a long and successful career as both a jockey and a trainer. He was lured out of retirement in 1971 to work for Penny Chenery at Meadow Stable. There, Lucien experienced success with Riva Ridge in 1972, and then Secretariat in 1973. With Lucien as trainer, he helped Meadow Stable become the number one stable in horse racing.

In the 2010 movie *Secretariat*, Lucien was portrayed by actor John Malkovich.

SECRETARIAT

Finally, a horse needs a talented jockey to guide them to victory. Secretariat (nicknamed "Big Red") had that in another Canadian, the great Ron Turcotte.[4]

---

[4]     Born in the Canadian province of New Brunswick, Ron Turcotte (born in 1941) is a Hall of Fame jockey. In a career that lasted nearly two decades, Ron won 3,032 races. Among those wins were six "Triple Crown" races. He rode Tom Rolfe to a win in the 1965 Preakness Stakes, before winning a combined five "Triple Crown" races aboard Riva Ridge and Secretariat in 1972 and 1973, respectively.

    Ron's career ended in 1978 when he fell from a horse during a race, causing paralysis. Since then, he has become an advocate for people with disabilities.

    In the 2010 movie *Secretariat*, Ron was portrayed by real-life jockey Otto Thorwarth.

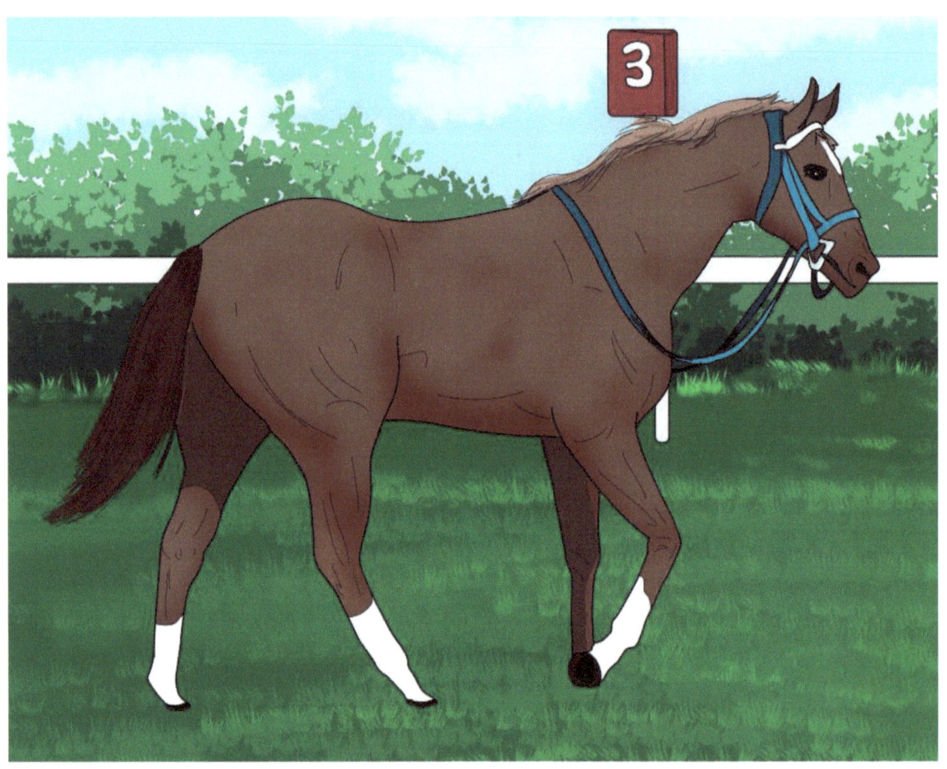
3

Born in 1970, Secretariat began his racing career in 1972. As a two-year-old, Big Red won seven of nine races, and was named American Horse of the Year.[5]

---

[5] Secretariat was born on March 30, 1970, at the Meadow Stable farm. His first race was on Independence Day (July 4), 1972, at Aqueduct Racetrack in Queens, New York. Due to a hard bump at the start of the race, Secretariat was only able to race back to a fourth-place finish. He finished first in his remaining two-year-old races, though he was disqualified to second (for interference) in one of them.

In a rare honor for a two-year-old, Secretariat was named American Horse of the Year in 1972.

# THOROUGHBRED PICAYUNE

### April 1973

SECRETARIAT UPSET;
FAVORITE PLACES 3RD
AT WOOD MEMORIAL;
FANS NOW CONCERNED
AS DERBY APPROACHES

Secretariat easily won his first two races of 1973, yet only finished third in his next race. Disappointed horse racing fans now began to question if he really was that good.[6]

________________________

[6] In the third race of Secretariat's 1973 season, he finished a disappointing third at the Wood Memorial Stakes, at Aqueduct Racetrack. This, after Secretariat had won his first two races of the season. It was later discovered that he had a large abscess in his mouth, which affected his performance. Because of the loss, it created concern for horse racing fans. After all, Secretariat's next race would be the Kentucky Derby.

5
6
10
11
12
IA

However, Secretariat silenced those doubters at the Kentucky Derby. Not only did Big Red win big, but he set a track record that still stands to this day.[7]

---

[7]  Secretariat's time at the 1973 Kentucky Derby was 1:59.4, a record that still stands. Held at Churchill Downs in Louisville, Kentucky, the race distance is 1.25 miles long. The Kentucky Derby is the first leg of the three "Triple Crown" races every year. Such races are reserved for three-year-old horses, which Secretariat was in 1973.

Then it was off to the Preakness Stakes, where again Secretariat won. And again, he set a track record. Sports fans everywhere were now following Big Red.[8]

---

[8] Secretariat's time at the 1973 Preakness Stakes was originally listed at 1:54.4. But years later, it was concluded that his time was in fact 1:53.0, which is now a record. Held at the Pimlico Race Course in Baltimore, Maryland, the race distance is just under 1.2 miles in length. The Preakness Stakes is the second of the three "Triple Crown" races every year.

Secretariat pleased those fans at the Belmont Stakes. He won horse racing's first Triple Crown in 25 years. It was yet another record, as he won by an unbelievable 31 lengths.[9]

---

[9]   Secretariat's time at the 1973 Belmont Stakes was 2:24.0. Held at Belmont Park in Elmont, New York, the racing distance is 1.5 miles. It is the third and final "Triple Crown" race every year. Secretariat's time remains a record for any 1.5-mile race on dirt. His 31-length margin of victory also remains a record for a "Triple Crown" race.

Secretariat's "Triple Crown" was the first for an American racehorse since Citation achieved that in 1948. It was thus the reprieve people in the United States needed. At the time, the country was troubled by the Vietnam War, the Cold War, a nationwide gasoline shortage, and the Watergate scandal. The latter issue would result in the 1974 resignation of U.S. President Richard Nixon.

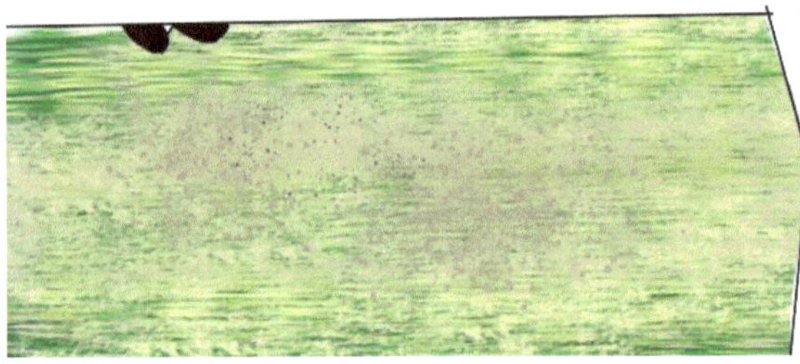

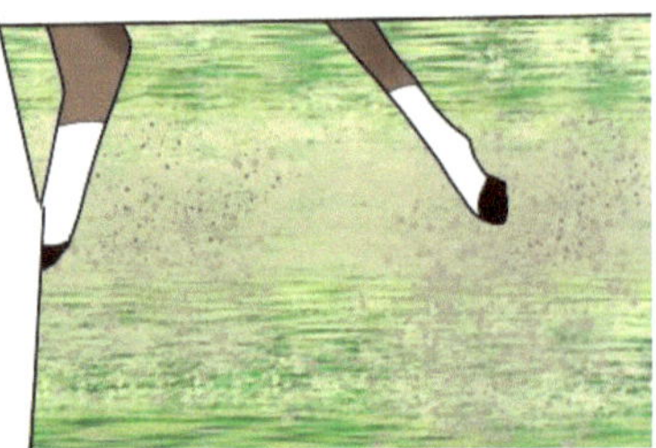

Shortly after winning the Triple Crown, Secretariat ran his last race in Toronto, Canada. He won, of course, then ended 1973 with another American Horse of the Year award.[10]

---

[10]     Before the 1973 season, Secretariat was syndicated with 32 investors buying stock at a combined total of a then-record $6.08 million (the equivalent of $40.5 million in 2022 dollars). Penny maintained four stocks, as well as the horse. The syndication came with the agreement that Secretariat would be retired at the end of that season.

His last race was on October 28, 1973. It was against older horses at the Canadian International Stakes at Woodbine Racetrack, in the Canadian city of Toronto, Ontario. Ron Turcotte was suspended due to a rules violation from a prior race with a different horse, so Eddie Maple took over as jockey. Secretariat won the event, his ninth of the season and 16th in 21 career races. He proved himself to be a versatile horse by winning races not only on dirt, but also on grass (like the one in Toronto).

During Secretariat's career, he earned $1.31 million ($8.78 million in 2022 dollars). He won his second American Horse of the Year award in 1973. Afterwards, Secretariat was retired to Claiborne Farm near Paris, Kentucky, where he was a favorite among its visitors.

# THOROUGHBRED PICAYUNE

October 1989

SECRETARIAT, 1970-1989
RACING GREAT DIES AT 19,
HOOF CONDITION BLAMED;
WON TRIPLE CROWN IN '73;
WAS LOVED BY EVERYONE

When Secretariat died in 1989, the grieving sports world mourned his loss. Yet he lives on in so many people, as one of the greatest racehorses who ever lived.[11]

---

[11] Near the end of his life, Secretariat suffered from a painful disease called laminitis, which affects the hooves, or the feet of horses and cattle. It made standing up very difficult at times for the horse. Finally, the decision to euthanize (or end the life of) Secretariat was made. It was done with dignity, to spare the horse from further suffering. Secretariat was 19 years old when he died on October 4, 1989. His life was the second-shortest lived of all Triple Crown winning horses from America who are now deceased. Secretariat is buried at Claiborne Farm, and is still visited by fans who wish to pay their respects.

In 2010, the Disney film company released the movie *Secretariat*. Trolley Boy and Longshot Max were the horses mainly used for Secretariat's role. It introduced him to a new generation of fans, many of whom weren't born when he lived. The movie thus ensured that the memory of Secretariat will live on.

## ABOUT THE AUTHOR

A.J. Chilson was born in Dallas, Texas in 1984. He has overcome childhood obstacles to become a poet, and then an award-winning author. This is A.J.'s 20th children's book. He currently lives and works in Winnsboro, Texas.

## ABOUT THE ILLUSTRATOR

Earl Haughton is an illustrator living in Jamaica, having illustrated around 100 books. This is his eighth book in collaboration with A.J. Chilson. Earl's passions outside of illustrating are his two daughters and the Arsenal Football Club.

## RESOURCES

- *Secretariat: The Making of a Champion* by William Nack
- *The Horse God Built* by Lawrence Scanlan
- *Secretariat: Racing's Greatest Triple Crown Winner (Thoroughbred Legends)* by Timothy M. Capps

www.ingramcontent.com/pod-product-compliance
Lightning Source LLC
Chambersburg PA
CBHW041636110726
48005CB00002B/620